THE ALCHEMY OF MY MORTAL FORM

Also by Sandy Longhorn

Blood Almanac
Anhinga Press

The Girlhood Book of Prairie Myths
Jacar Press

THE ALCHEMY OF MY MORTAL FORM

Poems by Sandy Longhorn

Winner of the 2014 Louise Bogan Award
for Artistic Merit and Excellence

Longhorn, Sandy
1st edition.

ISBN: 978-0-9855292-7-7
Library of Congress Control Number: 2014954703

Interior Layout by Lea C. Deschenes
Cover Design by Dorinda Wegener
Cover Art by Carolyn Guinzio
Editing by Tayve Neese and Issa Lewis

Printed in Tennessee, USA
Trio House Press, Inc.
Ponte Vedra Beach, FL

To contact the author, send an email to tayveneese@comcast.net

TABLE OF CONTENTS

GENERAL ORDERS

MY MORTAL FORM

GLOSSARY

GENERAL ORDERS

11 General Orders of a Whitecoat

Approach the body by preying without distinction.

Harass the union of disease, the army of invaders.

Root out the pickets, scouts, foraging parties.

Use the greatest vigor of movement in the attack.

Sacrifice the body in order to find what may be saved.

Form rotations to battle the degenerate blackness of night.

Expect profound repercussions at daybreak.

Lance the wounds & let the poison seep.

Acknowledge some good blood may be lost in the preservation.

Be vigilant. Watch for signs of a stalled heart.

Keep the weapon at the ready, a loud report to shock the pulse.

11 General Orders of a Nurse

Take charge of this fevered body and its possessions.

Walk the floor in a medical manner, antiseptic & mask at the
ready.

Report all violations of temperature or pulse, the staggered
breathing.

Become a pure conduit of the prescription without question.

Give over the pen, the chart when the clock relieves.

Transmit all orders & incidents to whomever follows,
offering the code.

Talk to no one except in the line of duty, conversation
a distraction ill afforded.

Press the red intercom of alarm only on the hint of death,
as in a fire raging in the blood.

Call the whitecoat listed in the book of hours for events
not covered here.

Attend all whitecoats who may appear, even unscheduled,
keeping eyes downcast & humble.

Be most watchful at night, a time of challenge when the body
senses any lapse and the fever leaps by degree.

11 General Orders of a Mystic

Make of your body a camouflaged shell.

Carry the sacred & the sacramental at all times hidden within.

Wear the mission sign on the left collar to be known one
    to the other.

Praise the tools assigned, their daily god-shapes.

Approach the fevered body as one approaches a trapped
    & rabid animal.

Hide the miniature shrine behind the headboard.

Speak in tongues, coded spells, an ash-coated whisper.

Enter the practiced trance to channel both strength & grace.

Use the force deemed necessary to compel compliance
    should the subject be unwilling.

Report all episodes of a body defiant.

Beckon the patient be penitent.

MY MORTAL FORM

FEVERS OF A MINOR FIRE

August, near the First

Dear Madame—

I address you with a tongue calloused
& lumbering. Imagine the skein of my hair,
humble & falling, neck ravaged.
Based on your favored advice,

I have passed some days burning
the locked boxes my suitors sent me.
The firelight refracted by the fever flush,
sweat on my brow & collarbone.

There is a feral oath in my throat,
dear Lady, I confess it.
I have pilfered many ounces of blood
from my heart & placed them in the vial.

In the fire, the garnet fluid boils,
holy & unholy, still. I have no prayers,
but my bruised veins pulse beneath
slack skin, pale & thin muscle cover.

Madame, will you answer only this?
The voice that steals along these walls
& calls me to the flame, is it you speaking?
It is a sweet & viscous sound, like the port

I sip each night to bring me sleeping.
I await your reply. Do not be hurried.
There is tinder enough to keep the fire
& plenty of red meat to replenish the heart.

—Your Subservient

The Alchemy
of My Mortal Form

I have hoarded my scars, kept accurate account
of rashes, wounds, & spells of amnesia.

The records state I am salt deficient & subject
to a febrile habit. Each night, my lips split & peel.

Today, I am sin & ash. This muslin gown electric,
white, a garment more apt for entry into paradise.

If confession be one part of the prescription,
I do confess. I have transgressed. I left the woman

I called *mother* the task of broom & dish rag.
I made of my soul a harbor for ill-will when asked

to forgive. I beg you, my whitecoat, draw the curtain.
The nurses may serve as our chorus of disregard.

Their backs turned, their hands tending patients
more likely to recover. Hurry. There is a panther

in the undertow of this fever. Its claws are laced
with radium, its jaw two racks of knives thirsty

for muscle & arterial blood. Do not trust the pulse.
I wait for you to save me, to wield the burning scythe.

THIS GARDEN
OF MY FRAGILE BREATH

August

Dear Madame—

Your presence is requested.
My throat narrows, my lungs
twin sisters of despair.

You think me overzealous?
I covet your breath, the ease
with which you part your lips.

The nurses here are vigilant, yes.
They test the tank for leaks,
the tubing for obstructions.

I find it mysterious, focus
instead on the garden's green
plumage. It swaggers & blooms

to satisfy my nerves. Each stalk
an altar, each petal an homage
to what travels on the air

through the lungs, into the blood.
The pollen glitters & corrupts.
I relish the gold salt of it,

the taste of a life force dwelling
on my tongue. I sip. I sup.
The nurses shake their heads,

take the stems away. Madame,
I await your arrival, the touch
of your glossy lips to my brow.

—*Your Sickling*

THE WINE SHOWS A BLOOD SHEEN

Above this metal bed, there is a window.

I arc & crane for a view of the boxed sky,
      the geese that burn an arrow pointing south.

The mystics bring red wine each night
      with meals of seared meat, raw in the fleshy center.

These succulents are meant to ease me into sleep.

The blood they draw from my arm is kin
      to what I drink & eat.

At night, I sense the wolves, their paws
      threading through the trees.

I do not fear their teeth. The prints they leave are key.

The whitecoats prescribe more medications meant
      to hold me here, their fragile fool. I play the part

but listen for the geese, the heavy-breathing wolves.
      I know the number of days before the moon darkens.

Tongueless, I Conjure Her at Will

August

Dear Madame—

The woman I called *mother* by mistake
brought me here when the sickness

made me shiver even in a scalding bath.
The water lapped the edges, spilled

in a cataract to the clean-tiled floor.
It soaked the towels there.

She dried me with rough care & bore
the weight of me to get my body here.

There is nothing in this room that smells
of her, though I request chrysanthemums,

let my fingers trail through their thick heads.
I bring the musk to my mouth, breathing

in such a way, I might drown on the scent.
I do not begrudge her leaving.

I saw her eyes when my lips formed the word.
We both knew I was orphaned then.

—Your Refugee

I Have Gone Shimmering into Ungentle Sleep

This fever is my tutor. It lectures
scarlet on my cheeks, pale quarter-moons

on all my fingernails, a heart that gallops beneath
the cold sting of stethoscopes unleashed.

I repose & ripen with the weight of secrets,
for I swore an oath to silence.

This bed my penitentiary, though
my chains pointless, cotton-woven.

Lethargy of limbs another symptom
pressed into the chart. The noise of the pen

blisters the brain. The catheter in the vein
delivers ruination, dreams induced to knock

my damaged crown askew. When I wake, my bones
have been replaced with porcelain, sinew

altered to wire, & my tongue, my tongue
lets loose what once was barred & guarded.

SEIZED WITH A SMALL FEVER

The linen here is burgundy, well-laundered.

My body, a vessel amended, rests
beneath a chandelier dimmed to sweetness.

The whitecoats prescribe meat laced with antipyretics.

I do my best to chew the sinew at the bone.
I do my best to improve.

Another, my mysterious, suggests I whisper my transgressions:

To have grown whole again after the breach, apology
withheld, tethered to a tongue rich with fat & salt.

From the shadows, she urges me. I resume:

To have a purse bursting with coins I've hoarded,
the luxury of silk & hibiscus petals.

Her breath bridles my neck. My lips persist:

To have chosen solitude & a bed of plumes,
of skin perfumed in ancient, secret oils.

The whitecoats arrive in lockstep. They ply my lips

with medicinal ice chipped to slivers. My mysterious,
my sorceress, hints that I am healing.

You Taught Me Devastation

End of August

Dear Madame—

I confess, the brutal cargo carried in my veins
scuttles my breath, an illness indecipherable,

the diagnosis gone astray. The whitecoats
shake their heads & my heart is a saber of shame.

I cling to chaos at your direction. Find no
pattern in the blossom of whistles let loose

by the attached machines that try to track me,
to trace each rise & fall of good cells versus bad.

They fail. At night, I return to your tutorage.
Recite the root causes of loss: *flame, water, wind, & ice.*

There is no trumpet song of triumph for those
lost in the delta of disease. We crouch in shadows,

in the never-fully-dark. Madame, I beseech you.
Send on the next lesson. My exhaustion is complete.

—Your Studious

Over Which a Feast Weight Passes

Two days after the fever breaks,
the mystics return with flanks of meat.

Fat & juice congeal on the plate.
The wine has been replaced.

A cup of milk squats on the tray.
Ice cold. A slip of froth.

They send another of their order
to manipulate slack limbs.

The spell she chants implores
the building back of muscle & bone.

Her breath is sweet with mint.
I keep my lips clamped tight.

Bits of meat rot between my teeth.
My body protests at the joints,

my head too heavy to be raised
from the pillow, hair grown threaded

through to knots. I am a rooted thing,
blood grown sluggish & mute.

This Vigil I Keep for Comfort

These hands cradle the fragments
of hushed gestures. They possess
a stammer & a tremble,

as if hooves beat in the veins
that map what moves beneath
the blazing skin. Every breath

is a reminder of the body
in exile, the compass dropped
down a dried-up well.

In the background, the machines
whir & bleat while the whitecoats
squander their smooth voices,

ordering higher doses, another
sting of the needle's tongue.
I bow down to gold-leafed grief.

The nurses are my anchors,
guard me from the leap at the lip
of the abyss. I claim a dumb tongue,

let my eyelids be sewn shut against
the surge of light. This vigil
needs no voice, no sight,

needs only the muted clamor
of nerves that signal pain
to an obedient brain.

Having Been Outside the Body

September

Dear Madame—

The progress of August is past.
The chart reads *relapse.*

On one upper arm a mulberry bruise
the size of my fist. A falling.

Trust that I have learned to leave this body.

I settle like a small furred creature in the corner
& observe. The white-shoed feet shuffle through.

The mystics have me on a starving diet, thin
slip of soup, a thimble of juice.

An experimental virus may be the cure.

From the windowsill I might see what new prescription
waits for me. Sometimes I scurry there, perch

on pink feet & nose the antiseptic air.
No one notices what is silent & soft.

Let the body on the bed bellow & writhe.

Let the whitecoats rush about, plunging their needles
into the veins. Let the pain reach its peak.

I will outlast the furnace blast.

I wait for your arrival, *Madame*.
The waiting brings me strength.

—*Your Resilient*

To Tamper & Tame Me
Piece by Piece

Whitecoats plot behind charts burgeoning
with tissue-thin papers, etched results
of specimens removed from the body-rubble.

Nurses blot out the sun & still I burn with drought.
The nutrients they introduce by pill, by drink,
by IV, all leach out of me in the fevered sweat.

I glow a bit, I think, although they've wrapped
my eyes with gauze for my own protection.
I feel the pulse of sirens in my blood, the throb

of an alien music. There are restraints
at my wrists & ankles to protect against
the wanderlust. Soon, I know, I must

find a way to circumvent their orders, to rise
from this bed & ease through the cracks
in the fortress wall. Surely, I grow thin enough.

THE ASHES OF MY FAMILIAR

Another woman kept this room before me,
I am sure. There is a husk of her temper yet

that rides the air. When I breathe in the burnt
remains, a strengthening returns. Rest assured,

we are conjoined in anonymity, although I learned
she died with her eyes open, if the nurses may be trusted.

When the whitecoats come, I invoke the posture
of the pasture, a flat expanse they trample

in the search for the root of my disease. The charm
is in the way they wring their hands when I ask after

my pretty predecessor. I've found a strand or two
of her red, red hair, cradled now & hidden well,

the beginning of a new concoction self-prescribed.
If I could find a fingernail or the remnant of a ribbon

used to lace her nightshirt closed, I would be closer
to the completion of my healing. I live to see the day

the whitecoats arrive to find me unwavering
in my form, the day I stand before them, whole,

& walk away with the shadow of my bedmate,
my mysterious, my true physician who does no harm.

Long Sliding Toward Oblivion

October, perhaps mid-month

Dear Madame—

There is news. A range of mystics has arrived.
They shuffled me off to a sepia room.

The tapestries here take the poison I give the air,

a sieve for my restless breath. A Lord & Lady,
their court & their menagerie, hover

while the mystics whipstitch airy spells.

I sup on the root of a dormant rumor, strange
tasting sedative, but sure. I clutch a shroud

of lofty linen, a cloth most apt at consolation.

Still, I am bewildered by your absence
as the incense whittles itself to ash.

The Lord & Lady wear their masks of disregard,

the mystics' lips are murmur-laden.
What must I do to beckon you here?

— Your Grappling Hook

Some Forgotten Fever

The bed is made of iron, flat
& straight. My cursive spine
breaks the line. To sleep, I turn

on my side, wake to shoulder
& arm aching. I rub the blood
back to life. The sharper wounds

I know sever my breath.
This is the hint of extinction
coaxed away like smoke drifting.

Yet in every exhale there remains
a small forgotten fever that ruins
muscle & bone & sweat-stained skin.

Left a Refugee Here
in a Sterile Country

When the fever shifts & loosens,
I understand absence, being born again
to solitude, the population of my hallucinations

elusive & in hiding. It is then,
when I think of the woman I called *mother*
by mistake & yearn for the soft yarn of her sweater,

the gloved hand taking mine
on the icy path, the way her lips were firm
in their enunciation of my name, though never *daughter*.

Once, when I was still a child,
she hoisted me into the low branches,
her arms sturdy as the thick limb that held me.

I never doubted her power
of protection, the way she lured the bees
away with a pot of sugared water or kept the stray

dogs at bay with a stick
kept ever at the ready. I know she wept
when she brought me here because the nurses tell me.

They beg to know her name,
a number or address, but I press my lips,
jaw clamped tight on the only lucid secret I have left.

We Live in Black & White

November

Dear Madame—

Be on your guard. There are secrets here
which I will seal with glue & string.

The woman I called *mother* by mistake takes pity,
sends me gifts addressed by an anonymous hand.

She keeps her name well-hidden from the whitecoats.
Though they wish to track her down & pull

some quantity of that bold liquid from her veins,
they are mistaken in their belief of our relation.

If you know her whereabouts, assure her I am mute.

She sends photos from my youth in careful order,
posing & reposing me in a healthy body.

Why, in several shots I'm fairly blurry from the motion
of my limbs. There! Her shadow lingers in each frame,

her ardor a beaked thing that plucked at me.
We were a pleated pair. Our scarves charted

the catastrophe of wind as we walked
the ice-path home. Her gloved hand held me firm.

Please, *Madame*, find her. Tell her I am resolute.

—Your Beggar

Inside, the Ice Assembles

The nurses say the seasons turn.
I see little but one squat square of sky.

On days when the fever lets loose of me,
I notice the gathering clouds, the way

their weight shifts toward snow. Several
mornings have seen frost upon the glass.

A message pressed in intersecting crystal lines.
Perhaps a map. An aerial view. It fades

so fast in the sun. I confess, I've wept
with the frustration of my reading corrupted

by the melt. Water, like blood, an infirm medium.
The whitecoats order thermal blankets

when chills erupt from my shoulders,
shaking the bed along my weakened spine.

They want a curtain for the ill-sealed window
but I refuse it. They do not understand

my body's desire. The wings I used to know,
absent now. Hollowed bones echoing

the memory of wind. By instinct, I gauge
distances, updraft, thermals, but am resigned,

rooted. This body would not rise, even if
I could hurl it into the freezing air.

The Calendar is Turned, the Year Anointed

January, the First

Dear Madame—

They've wrapped my eyes with gauze
        forcing the lids closed
                against the fevered light.
They've swaddled my arms to my chest,
        attached more tubing & alarms.
I dictate these words in an empty room,
              where they fall
      to damp sheets & dissolve.
I know by the sound of footsteps
        & the rustle of starched cotton
when to let my lips
      flutter to a close. I separate the whitecoats
        from the nurses by each touch,
              each breath.
     One has fingers smooth as the piano keys
in the great arcade;
        one rough calloused skin that abrades.
    Their breath brings coffee,
           mints, stagnant meat.
Madame, I am hollowed & hallowing.
       They say the symptoms
    returned on the solstice. I grew aggressive
in my agitation,
        became the bird that hurls itself
against the pane, threatened by its own reflection.
      They say I drew blood,
    but I cannot find the scars.

Minus fingers, I memorize these lines & channel
your voice,
chanting in the dark.

—*Your Immovable*

A Dark, Gelatinous Ruin

Before the fever replenishes & returns,
the pain advances on the hollow space
behind each eye. Blacksmiths pound
the anvils there, & my pulse betrays me,
this clenched jaw, a dead giveaway.

Do not believe that my begging for alms,
for the withheld balm, means I haven't
sacrificed, haven't cried out on the pyre
of prayers in penance. Despite the doubt
written on the whitecoat's face, on my chart,

I try to heal myself. I promise to purge
reticent cells, pledge allegiance to calcium
& iron, loose my grip on my disgrace, this blood
thinning, radiant in its desire to ruin, to creep
& seep along the pathways to my heart.

The whitecoat proclaims my body a stubborn
subject that refuses. He shakes his head, scolds.
Against my will, I wilt, weeping before him.
I suffer & succumb. This body now
his salvaged wreck to scavenge.

WHAT COLLECTS
IN THE DARK TUNNELS

The cold has settled in, the window wreathed
in crystals sharp as the ache in the bone of my hip
where the whitecoat scooped the marrow.

He was unshaven & disheveled, but his force
never faltered. His needle wide-mouthed & boring down.
The sample a mossy pink mass of transgressions.

Today they will begin the transfusion, a ritual
in transplantation meant to recall strength,
to waken slack muscles & this dulled brain.

A hulking form waits in the corner, hazy machine
poised on sturdy haunches, ready to speed
the clean blood's sleek descent. I confess,

I am thirsty for the thick crimson brew.
Do not think me traitorous to my own form.
I mean only to document the nicking of the vein,

the odd thrill of taking someone else's cells into my own.
Given by sinner or penitent, the garnet liquid glows.
I crave the chance to cradle it in my hands,

to hear it croon that I may feel enlivened by tomorrow,
that I may lift my body, may stand once again,
feeding on what will then be coursing through my limbs.

Vessel in Which
an Ancient Urge Rises

The furnace here is faulty, heaves a dry heat
past the needle of the thermostat.

My lips are prone to chap. At night, I peel
my cuticles, gnaw & pull, cannot resist

the little twinge of pain, the pearl of blood
I suck to detect some trace of the donor,

anonymous source that fed the tubes.
My intimate. My confessor.

I have never taken another body into my own.

This sharing of the vein is a cold science,
though I sweat – from furnace or fever

only the whitecoats know. The nurses bring me
lotion & balm, bandage my fingertips.

When the raw flesh cools, I cry, cut off
from the taste of my salvation.

THAT WHICH BLOOMS
BEYOND WHERE IT IS PLANTED

This new blood has taken root,
my donor replete & replicate.
I felt it first as a flutter in the womb,

then a surge of cells thickening,
an added weight drawing me back
to my own body. The confirmation

is in the whitecoats, their smiles,
their nods in the direction of nurses
who tend to linens & flesh. I confess,

I have admired the bodies of those
who crowd me, the effortless lifting
of a hand, the precision of a step.

I have wanted to rise among them.
Yet, I am become a host, fed upon,
overrun by what aims to heal me.

One whitecoat leans in, whispers,
Embrace the foreign bodies.
Incubate these alien, last-chance lives.

THE RADIANT SHIMMER OF SUPPLICATION

January at the close

Dear Madame—

Have you heard from her,
the woman I called *mother* by mistake?
She visits me at night, I swear it.

In the matted hours of the last new moon,
I heard a caterwaul outside my window,

the thrash of some wild creature
among dead stalks, caught in thorns.

Lately, in the first breach of light, I detect
thumbprints on the outside of the glass,
the hoarfrost of her breath.

I beg you, be munificent. Seek her out,
discover what message she has for me.

Tell her the script is severed by the sun,
the nurses with their pills, pink & white.

Tell her this new blood gilds my veins,
but I remain the same body. I beseech you.
Convey my regard & my devotion.

I grow steadfast in my determination
to find her in the world that follows this.

My signature is my token.

—Your Debtor

A Sluggish Dullness
Sacrificed or Shed

Six days have passed without a sign
        of fever. I keep my own chart,
pulling loose six fragile threads

from the frayed corner of the bed.
        For confirmation, I look sideways
at the pen, read the new results

in the number of strokes the nurses
        make on the page. I fear the whitecoats
do not trust me. Their lips refuse to move

to any mention of this remission. Needles
        still draw blood. I mourn the loss
of each drop, thicker now, a deeper

garnet since my donor's offer of salvation.
        Despite their doubt, I can attest my health.
My muscles bear it out. At night,

I slip from my bed to pace the confines
        of this room. I drag tubes like tendrils,
never stray farther than the reach

of the machines that would alert the nurses.
        I do simple calisthenics until a damp rises
on my skin, this the clean sweat

I've called up of my own volition.
        To calm the pulse, I stand beneath
my barred window, head tipped back

to track the moon's marking off of time,
        the subtle shifting of constellations. I plot.
I plan for my release into that faint light.

Resurrected as a Refugee

Monitor, needle, & chart,
each new diagnostic hints
that I am healing, though

the pattern must repeat
a longer cycle than the moon
going blank, then slowly filling,

before the whitecoats
will adjust the medications
downward, will begin to trust.

Then, this body will be weaned
from its sterile life-source
to see if health will hold.

I admit I feel the building back
of muscle layers, a throbbing
ache in shoulder, calf, & thigh.

No mystics needed now,
the donor cells are hearty,
loud-voiced workers hoisting

the weak & the dead, standing
in their stead. The donor infiltrates
my sleep. In the night I meet

a host of unfamiliar faces, a mass
of bodies beckoning. I transgress.
I take this family as my own.

Leering at My Lessened State

March, the first, more lamb than lion

Dear Madame—

The nurses bring a mirror in,
deem me fit to face the image

of a new body carved from the soft
curves, the plush excess I carried

before the fevers. I am hybrid now.
This donor-self sickly thin, a skin

that sags from shoulder knobs, hair
all split ends & ragged lengths.

The whitecoats order a mystic in.
Shears, soaps, lotions. Her hands

caress a rosy breath upon my cheeks,
a glow upon my brow, exposed

by a shorn scalp, damaged locks
cut away, unable to be saved.

Madame, who will come for me now,
transformed & unfamiliar?

—Your Constant in Disguise

THE BODY ITSELF THE NARRATOR OF THE MESSAGE

In the days of my healing, they sent a mystic
with a burning stick of incense. His tunic whispered

well-washed spells; his hands the beaks of two fast birds
that weaned me from my machines one needle at a time.

Red skin flared beneath his fingers as he swiped
at the adhesive. He lacked conviction, offered little

consolation beyond a raised brow. Yet, I have begun
to see the magic of his work. When the night nurse slips

under the charm of the late hour, I sneak past her
to enter the closest whitecoat's den. In the dim,

I touch his photographs, his bronze & silver
paperweights, the luxury of his leather chair. I leave

my offerings, a fingerprint placed over his name,
threads from the loose noose of my collar, a cuticle

torn with my teeth, the faintest drop of blood
still wet at the edge, proof of my newly mixed life.

These totems my prayer for early release, for the day
the tests no longer detect any trace of donor or of fever.

BRUISED, MY DARKER NATURE ENTERS ME

They say that they sedate me
to tap the mother lode of sleep.
They claim a smooth, mineral rest.

Little do they know, the brain refuses
while the body feigns, feints,

whittles away the hours of eyes
gauze-wrapped against
the frank, medicinal light.

In the never-fully dark, I plan
to stir the pot. I plot. I whisper

to the donor cells. I sing of union
& reunion, of mix & blend,
a dalliance of alliance, red web

of nutrients suckled & shared.
Yet, beneath the lowered heart rate,
within loose limbs, a rebel conversation

simmers. Given no choice, I gather
my donor close, make my enemy

my accomplice in the plans for escape.

Harboring the Remains
& the Many Etceteras

Slept hard. Sweated some.
Woke to a tongue dry, swollen.

With this new blood loping, doping
my veins, only my dreams remain

steeped in fever toxins. The poison
seeps in the dark, & the woman

I called *mother* by mistake watches
me wrestle an oversized steering wheel,

the car taking each rushing curve more sharply,
on the cusp of spinning from my control.

Strapped into the passenger seat, she remains
impassive as her features blur, melt

into a moon of semi-precious pebbles.
I am thrown through the windshield skyward.

All the syllables turn to glue in my throat.
I wake with arms outstretched,

unsure if I mean to ward off the threat
or gather in some comforting body.

What Rides
on that Swift Currency of Air

April

Dear Madame—

Finally, I comprehend the distance kept,
recognize each mystic sent as envoy.

They enter without speaking; their steps
measure the breadth, the depth of prayer.

One is tasked to wash my matted hair,
to cut away the knots. Her skin smells

of lavender & bread, your kitchen table.
Another arrives to sweep, then polish

the floor, the tiles already a blinding,
innocent white. She whistles our same

self-mocking tune. When the third arrives
to remove that hulk of a machine,

we exchange swift looks, pass messages on air.
His eyes cut from your glacial ice, the same

precise verdict. Your intent is clear.
Nourished & soothed, I am cocooned

but gaining. My limbs press the barriers,
muscles firm, nearly ready for the return.

—Your Tethered

Red & Reeling with the Journey

Three nights after the full moon passed
its white sleeve through the bars of my window,

I feel the first cramp in my belly. No, lower.
I catch the scent of blood. An old haunt returning.

Something I'd thought lost with the fever,
boiled to sediment & brushed away,

revisits the womb long empty. At dawn,
I'm forced to call the night nurse in, her eyes

still fixed with the caul of sleeping while charged
to duty. My tongue lolls, my lips unmoving.

I must point instead to the garnet blemish
stark against the bleached nightshirt.

Fetching whitecoats, she forms an assembly,
bends over the chart, scratches orders

for another vial of blood, more iron sulfate,
a mystic to palpate, question, & inspect.

I am resigned beneath their smiles, their wagging
heads, if not rejoicing. I worry for the loss,

the new-merged cells of donor & self,
the strength I had been gaining.

THE SLOW TONNAGE
OF MY PRIOR CRIME

Once, before this body failed, several suitors
courted me, interest they expressed
from a distance, eyes cast down,
gifts sent in locked boxes made of teak
varnished smooth as polished jewels,
cool beneath my grasping hands.

The woman I called *mother* by mistake
held the keys. I had to earn them,
charged to overcome my clumsy habits,
my appetite for sugar & bread, my body
heavy then, prone to stumble on any
exposed root, the garden hose, the stairs.

My flesh had grown dough soft & pale,
only my hands, my face exposed
to sun or another human pair of eyes.
I practiced being hidden, a living ghost
slouching through dim hallways, knocking
portraits askew as I hugged each paneled wall.

She begged me thin myself, practice balance,
but I never confessed to my transgressions,
the untamed lust for what would keep me plump.
The deeper crime was that I feared the men
circling my periphery. Our female house
was whole & hadn't failed me yet.

Awash in Hunger
for the Pistil & the Stamen

—after Emily Rosko

In the oceanic light, the atrium at night,

caught in the act, scissors & blooms,
   fingers stem-stained, thorn-stung,

I become marble skinned, a statuary body

amid the stalks, the dense green breath.
   Caught a temptress estranged,

muzzled, my wreath of flowers set afire,

the newly grafted & the heirloom strain
   dominion of the whitecoat's crown.

This hunger harvested from a year left fallow,

a body taper-thin, more vine than fruit-bearing flesh,
   an ache in the puckered pit that sent me

on my verdant mission. With tongue still tinged

gold, green, I am led away by the soft-soled sentry,
   returned infirm to the glare of my room,

the one window diamond-buffed & barred.

I, Who have been Pressed & Prettied

June

Dear Madame—

There is news.

I have walked the requisite number of steps
unaided. No line, no bead, no sweat

arose at my brow or lip. No stutter or sway
betrayed my hours of practice.

I have lifted my arms, my legs, dressed
myself in a light blouse, a pair of pants,

looking fairly human, if my hair
would grow back from the shear's hack.

I confess my feet resist the shoes, prefer
the comfort of skin meeting floor,

but the whitecoats frown, so I force
my toes, the arch, the heel to fit.

On my inch-thick chart, I spy the day nurse
noting the results. I deduce the numbers

for the blood's weight & core body temp
by the fact that I've passed this other test.

Still, the whitecoats warn, to be complete
I must give in to speech, must reveal

the name & numbers of the woman
to whom I will be released. I delay.

Will you send on your advice? I trust.

—*Your Strengthening*

Offered Passage, Offered Healing

When the mystic arrives to note my crimes,
she begins by clearing my throat of the threads
I swallowed to make a muting nest.

She hovers bedside, a levitating force
chanting her questions in loops & chains.
What have you done? What have you done?

Do you want to be released? Do you want
to be relieved? Do you want? She oil-anoints
my jaw; she cradles & she coaxes.

I cry out that I refused the gifts once offered
by the woman I called *mother* by mistake,
her home-grown meals & hand-sewn gowns.

I left three hearts behind heavy & scarred
when I learned which words bore the sharpest
edges, which could be both missive & missile.

In the testing time, I failed to conquer forgiveness,
my memory of the betrayal a sour fruit
I cultivated for a yearly feast. It grew & grew.

The mystic bows her head to transcribe, claims
purging holds the power of transcendence.
We are both waiting for the deepest, darkest.

SMALL-TIME RAPTURE

—after Mary Ann Samyn

June

Dear Madame—

The turning point was thus:

A mystic came with a styptic gaze,
a nervy mercy in the dose
of his testimony, unabridged.

Something winged & patented beat
beneath his skin. A trapped thing tapped.

I felt it during the laying on of hands,
the diagnostic & the blessing.

We grappled with predictions.

Friction & heat revealed the myths
born of fluctuations in the blood,
the membranes storing memories.

I watched the fine figure of his finger
trace the outline of my escape, a hatch

only I could open, the hinges rusted
& needy. The trick was to find

the correct grade of oil, which luster
could bracelet, slip, & seep into
those rough grooves, produce a loosening.

My sluggish ways no longer an option.

The answer is hidden in the rhetoric
of perk & pluck loud-throated.

My goal, my joy, to decipher the glossy reward.

—*Your Detective*

Let Loose in Blue & Green

Each day that I progress, I make some new
discovery. The fact is there are others here.

I hadn't thought, though now I hear the moaning
& the pleas when certain doors are opened.

I wonder if such sounds came out of me,
who recorded my existence then.

Another truth: there is a courtyard,
high-walled, bricked, windowless.

A mystic guards the gate, administers
my prescription, 20 minutes, once per day.

Alone, I make my circuit. The first dose
a mistake. I threw myself down on the grass,

the better to see that swath of blue, larger
than my window's allowance. The mystic

sounded the alarm. I was removed, learned
to keep my calm, work my legs at walking

round & round the square. My one tell,
the arc of my neck in the final moment, craned,

on the verge of pain, my feet stopped
not from weakness but from want.

To Taste the Sooty Tangle of her Signature

The woman I called *mother* by mistake
sends me secrets, envelopes addressed
by another's hand, letters arranged

in code, built of a script smudged hazy.
She tells me to divide my penance by
my punishment, meaning my prescription

when written in her tilt, her whorls.
She begs me approximate the blame,
the balance left in my body-ledger.

There is a temple beneath your heart, a shrine
sketched by scalpel and stitching thread
fine as the spider's cradle-web, she says.

No pill, no liquid injection will breach
the door. Only a diamond-bladed axe could
chop it out. I must remain resolved.

She requests a bit of fingernail, a drop
of newly concocted blood-sap dried on cloth,
any flicker of green, be it grass, stem, or leaf,

that has pressed my tongue. With these
she will string a microscopic instrument,
will predict the date of my release, my return.

The Body's Instinct is to Bloom

So, this is what it means
          to conquer the fire of fever,
to go days, weeks,
     & now months
                    without a sizzle
behind the tongue,
          beneath the skin,
drizzles of sweat no longer making rivulets
     along the throat's curve.

The body tamed is health.

          I must forgive the whitecoats
                    for how they forced
my hands to loose their hold
     on the pyrite & the flint.

I had grown so used to trafficking in ash.

The whitecoats saved the root of me,
     enough healthy flesh
                    kept hidden
          from the flames
to offer this rebirth,
     though I often fought their tugs,
                    their scrapes,
their marriage
          of brutal antiseptics
                    to this fiery pit.

Compliant now
         under their smooth-fingered grazing,
                  I allow them to lift,
pinch, & shift newly muscled limbs,

to persuade the new growth
                  forming on the budding branches.

Preparation
for the Transfer of Control

Today is marked for valuation, a day
to catalog my earthly estate. I am dressed
in donated clothes, cheap cloth that chafes

as I await the mystic's knock. This new act,
the request for permission to enter, does more
to buttress my belief in remission than all

the charted numbers once revealed.
When I grant entry, the mystic carries
a notebook, a tiny box, a plastic bag.

I offer up my few letters from the woman
I called *mother* by mistake, the papers crumpled,
lead-smudged; then, the dried remains

of flowers once pressed beneath my mattress.
She notes these in her book & opens the box
to reveal a silver necklace with a blue stone,

tells me this clung to my neck when I arrived.
Her hands are gentle, confident at the clasp.
The bag holds my old blouse & skirt,

too large now, the scent of fever clinging
to the seams. I dismiss the mystic & disrobe,
drape raw skin in the fabric's comfort.

Preparation
for the Moment of Escape

After the valuation,
        I withdraw the pilfered knife,
     return to the prying loose.
The window opens inward,
        a fatal flaw allowing
access to the bars & the mortar
     loosening around the screws.

The day I assessed the metal fatigued,
     more ornament than guard,
                I began.

        Now, I wrap my hands
   in strips of torn cloth
lest some scrape betray me.
     I'm nearly there & thankful
        for this body winnowed
   to a sapling width,
      easily slipped
through the gap, a weight
     light enough to drop
        to the cradling bushes.

My one regret,
    that I won't see their faces
        when they knock & wait
& eventually discover this room
             emptied
of a now-hale body, emptied
    of all my small possessions,
       save the stub of this dulled knife.

Cloaked in Darkness
& in Health

June

Dear Madame—

I send this letter in advance of my escape.

The whitecoats hint at my release but offer
only obstacles. Their latest word is *destitute.*

A mystic offers up the ledger of my debts.

My sins have stretched the leather, the spine
imperiled by the list of potions & procedures.

When my body burned beneath their hands,

when my veins resisted their prescriptions,
the whitecoats found me fashionable, a test

of their true aptitudes, a quest to set their names

in bold font, spinning through the profession. But,
I am passing wholesome now, have become

a burden taking up a bed with no means

for repayment. I will not demean the woman
I called *mother* by mistake by revealing her.

I refuse the mystic's pleading & her threats.

Each night, I work more quickly at loosening
the bars at the window. Each day, I memorize

the path I'll take. Expect me three nights past

the new moon. I'll be insolvent, hungry,
in need of just enough to make my way.

—*Your Fixed & Penniless*

GLOSSARY

To Parse, *To Save,*
One Must State the Relevant

Deliver, rescue, or protect the body from the marrow,
         from the rising again of fever flush & sweat.

Reclaim the personhood from corruption, hallucinations
         put to rest beside the curses, the threats, the wailing.

Allow to live, spare the veins from poison, the blood
         from thinning beyond the capillaries' capabilities.

Reserve, store up, put by the healthy cells, teach the body
         to accept this sustenance, this redemption.

Keep secure, cherished, & well-guarded the prescription,
         the medicinal vials, the name of the donor.

Prevent the opposition, that disease that dodged all diagnoses,
         from making a return, meaning carry out the cure.

THE DEFINITION OF A FEBRILE *BODY*

Flesh, as opposed to soul or spirit,
become an instrument of heat,
the material being, the main portion
a tract for flames in the veins
or running along the false-red skin.

The nave of a church in a hot country,
all waxen melt & sun-stained pews;
the hull of a ship run aground
at the equator, wooden planks, pitted
with salt & sand, meeting the tide;
the load-bearing part of any vehicle
straining against the weight, burning
out whatever engine churns beneath;
the central text caught up in the hands
of the zealot & tossed on the bonfire.

A force fit for fighting, the assemblage
bearing torches on the long march
with oil & embers raining down
to scar hands, arms, faces.
A piece of matter, a bulk, solid & full
of flavor, sweat that stings with toxic
spices leached from the blood.

A not-yet-corpse composed of its own
pyre, fuse, & unstruck match.

THE SICKLY *MARROW* DEFINED

What lurks *in the cavities of bones, a soft vascular
substance,* in this patient-case, no longer vital,

gone weak with fever & a leaching sweat.

What *the body feeds on,* all rich nutrition self-made
& self-proclaimed, yet muted in this body

to a sticky, whispered mass of not-quite cells.

What *fills the spinal cord,* separate from the other,
the long cylindrical life-force wilting under the glare

of needles & medicinal lights left on all night.

Of her *vegetal nature,* her *pith & pulp* desiccated
by the body-drought. *The vital essential part*

of new growth sapped of the will to reproduce.

What they dream of in their whitecoated sleep.
A mossy pink quicksand, lava-hot, sucking

them under, patient & practitioner alike.

TRANSFORMATION, DEFINITIVE NOTES FROM A LEARNÈD HAND

The action of changing in form, a metamorphosis.
    In the patient, there are two—
        the coming on of sickness
        the commencement of healing
    Often the reversal is minute,
        more than microscopic
        over weeks or months
    Often the patient loses patience

Another variation, a complete conversion of character.
    There may be wailing, lashing out,
        teeth bared, the bite aggressive
    There may be silence

An entity transcended in accordance with a set of rules.
    The governance remains mysterious,
        a formula of poke & prod, slice & stitch
        a drawing out, a pouring in of fluids
    The prescription modified on a suspicion,
        a curtain-shrouded secret

The genetic alteration of a cell, introduction of donor DNA.
    This the splice & graft by absorption—
        layer in the healthy on the lethal
        stand by, wait,
        hovering is useless

HEALTH, AN EXPANDED DEFINITION

Sound condition of the body
> as in able to lift the wet laundry, to pin
> the full-grown heft of it to the line;
> as in legs that could brace for & bear
> the weight of any ordinary burden;
> as in the will to scab, to seal over
> the minor wounds rather than to fester.

Freedom from disease
> wherein the body remains temperate,
> modulating the heating, the cooling airs;
> wherein the throat refuses the hoarse voice
> of swollen glands & fever flush;
> wherein joints prevail, smooth movers
> well-oiled, the stiff seizing curtailed.

Vim & vigor
> the three-pronged pulse, a steady study
> under normal conditions, fit to rear up,
> to race when stirred by the beauty
> of another body, capable of calming
> to the languid slur of well-earned sleep;
> a zealous mass of cells at the ready.

Spiritual or moral soundness
> what was feared given up or lost
> in the inertia, that loosening of the spine;
> what will be a crucial element of the cure,
> the reason for the mystery & the mystics;
> what the body bends to pray for,
> daily oblations to a tight-lipped god.

Acknowledgments

Grateful acknowledgment is made to the editors and readers of the following journals in which poems in this collection have appeared or are forthcoming, sometimes in slightly different form:

32 Poems: "The Ashes of My Familiar"

Anti-: "The Alchemy of My Mortal Form"

Barn Owl Review: "Awash in Hunger for the Pistil & the Stamen" and "Small-Time Rapture"

Bellevue Literary Review: "To Parse, *To Save,* One Must State the Relevant"

Bluestem: "Seized with a Small Fever"

burntdistrict: "11 General Orders of a Nurse" and "The Calendar is Turned"

Cant Journal: "Leering at My Lessened State" and "Preparation for the Transfer of Control"

Connotation Press: "I, Who have been Pressed & Prettied," "Offered Passage, Offered Healing," "Red & Reeling from the Journey," and "*Transformation,* Definitive Notes from a Learnèd Hand"

Copper Nickel: "11 General Orders of a Mystic" and "Over Which a Feast Weight Passes"

Crazyhorse: "We Live in Black & White"

diode: "The Body Itself the Narrator of the Message" and "*Health,* an Expanded Definition"

Grist: "This Vigil I Keep for Comfort"

Hayden's Ferry Review: "I Have Gone Shimmering into Ungentle Sleep" and "Left a Refugee Here in a Sterile Country"

Hotel Amerika: "A Dark, Gelatinous Ruin"

Linebreak: "Fevers of a Minor Fire"

North American Review: "Having Been Outside the Body"

Pamplemousse: "Bruised, My Darker Nature Enters Me," "Harboring the Remains & the Many Etceteras," and "Cloaked in Darkness & in Health"

Redactions: "Some Forgotten Fever"

The Southeast Review: "The Definition of a Febrile *Body*"

Sou'wester: "To Tamper & Tame Me Piece by Piece"

Thrush: "You Taught Me Devastation"

Tupelo Quarterly: "The Body's Instinct is to Bloom" and "That Which Blooms Beyond Where it is Planted."

"Small-Time Rapture" appeared on *Verse Daily*.

"Fevers of a Minor Fire" and "Having Been Outside the Body" appeared in *Poets on Growth* from Math Paper Press

This book would not have been possible without the generous support of *Trio House Press,* with special thanks to Tayve Neese, Issa Lewis, and Dorinda Wegener.

All my thanks go to Carol Frost for selecting this book.

Thanks as well to my colleagues at Pulaski Technical College for their continued belief in my work.

The writing of these poems would not have been possible without the writings of Emily Dickinson, Lucie Brock-Broido, Mary Ann Samyn, and Lisa Russ Spaar.

As ever, you who are my friends and family sustain me.

And, of course, Chuck West, nobody does it better, makes me feel sad for the rest. Thank you for giving me the space and time to write and for all of your love.

About the Author

Sandy Longhorn is also the author of *The Girlhood Book of Prairie Myths*, winner of the 2013 Jacar Press Full Length Poetry Book Contest, and *Blood Almanac*, winner of the 2005 Anhinga Prize for Poetry. Longhorn holds a Master of Fine Arts degree in poetry from the University of Arkansas and a Bachelor of Arts degree in English from the College of St. Benedict. She has worked in bookselling and in publishing in the past and now teaches at Pulaski Technical College, where she directs the Big Rock Reading Series, and for the online MFA Program at the University of Arkansas Monticello. In addition, she co-edits the journal *Heron Tree* and blogs at *Myself the only Kangaroo among the Beauty*.

About the Artist

Carolyn Guinzio is a poet and photographer living in Fayetteville, Arkansas. Her most recent collection is *Spoke & Dark* (Red Hen, 2012)

About the Book

The Alchemy of My Mortal Form was designed at Trio House Press through the collaboration of:

Tayve Neese, Lead Editor
Issa Lewis, Supporting Editor
Carolyn Guinzio, Cover Art
Dorinda Wegener, Cover Design
Lea Deschenes, Interior Design

The text is set in Adobe Caslon Pro.

The publication of this book is made possible, whole or in part,
by the generous support of the following individuals and/or agencies:

Anonymous

About the Press

Trio House Press is a collective press. Individuals within our organization come together and are motivated by the primary shared goal of publishing distinct American voices in poetry. All THP published poets must agree to serve as Collective Members of the Trio House Press for twenty-four months after publication in order to assist with the press and bring more Trio books into print. Award winners and published poets must serve on one of four committees: Production and Design, Distribution and Sales, Educational Development, or Fundraising and Marketing. Our Collective Members reside in cities from New York to San Francisco.

Trio House Press adheres to and supports all ethical standards and guidelines outlined by the CLMP.

The Editors of Trio House Press would like to thank Carol Frost.

Trio House Press, Inc. is dedicated to the promotion of poetry as literary art, which enhances the human experience and its culture. We contribute in an innovative and distinct way to American Poetry by publishing emerging and established poets, providing educational materials, and fostering the artistic process of writing poetry. For further information, or to consider making a donation to Trio House Press, please visit us online at: www.triohousepress.org.

Other Trio House Press Books you might enjoy:

What the Night Numbered by Bradford Tice
>2014 Trio Award Winner selected by Peter Campion

Your Immaculate Heart by Annmarie O'Connell, 2014

Flight of August by Lawrence Eby
>2013 Louise Bogan Winner selected by Joan Houlihan

The Consolations by John W. Evans
>2013 Trio Award Winner selected by Mihaela Moscaliuc

Fellow Odd Fellow by Steven Riel, 2013

Clay by David Groff
>2012 Louise Bogan Winner selected by Michael Waters

Gold Passage by Iris Jamahl Dunkle
>2012 Trio Award Winner selected by Ross Gay

If You're Lucky Is a Theory of Mine by Matt Mauch, 2012